SCREEN STARS

BY RUSSEL

SCREEN STARS ®

ULTRAWEIGHT
XL/TG (46-48)

SUN UNLIMITED
LOS ANGELES, CALIF

STYLE 606

anvil
PRE-SHRUNK -L-
100% COTTON
FABRIC MADE IN U.S.A.
ASSEMBLED IN HONDURAS
OVER FOR CARE

WEAR-GUARD®
RUGGED CLOTHES
MADE IN U.S.A.
STYLE 606   SIZE XL
CARE & CONTENT ON REVERSE

DRY CLEAN ONLY
SLEEPING BAG RECORDS
974 BROADWAY NY, NY 10025

QualiTee's
ONLY THE BEST
100% COTTON
MADE IN U.S.A.   XXL

XL 50% COTTON
50% POLYESTER
Made in U.S.A.
CARE ON REVERSE SIDE
SCREEN STARS

9 oni ™
BY Tee Jays
100% COTTON
EXTRA HEAVYWEIGHT
MADE IN U.S.A.

Ta
BROOKLYN, N.Y.
XXL

RY
MADE IN CANADA
FABRIQUÉ AU CANADA
50% COTTON/COTTON
50% POLYESTER
AC 46

Stedman®
Made in USA
XL
(46-48) 50% Kodel & Polyester
50% Cotton

PEM
GREAT ENTERTAINMENT
MERCHANDISE INC
XL

BACKSTAGE PASS
L/G
XL/TG

TULTEX
Large
Grande/G and

Sport-Tee
Americana LTD.
M
RN 81182
100% COTTON

L 100% COTTON
TEE BEST
PRE-SHRUNK
Made in Honduras

XXXL Made in U.S.A.
100% COTTON
CARE ON REVERSE SIDE
SCREEN STARS ®

ACTIVEWEAR
100% COTTON PRE-S
ASSEMBLED IN MEXICO FROM U
X-LARGE

RN 78349 XL
T-AMERICA
PRE-SHRUNK
100% COTTON
Made in Honduras

L COTTON
CARE ON REVERSE SIDE
VECTA

FIVE STAR
100% COTTON M
RN 96050
MADE IN PAKISTAN

touch of gold
by
Spring Ford XL
100% COTTON
fabric made in U.S.A.
ASSEMBLED IN MEXICO

TOP

White House ™
S
50% POLYESTER 50% COTTON
MADE IN U.S.A.

BAY CLUB
XL
100% COTTON
RN 7570
MADE IN PANAMA
REVERSE FOR CARE

THE PADDINGTON CORPORATION
100% COTTON
MADE IN CHINA
ONE SIZE FITS A
COVER FOR CARE

PFD
A
AA
ALSTYLE APPAREL
& ACTIVEWEAR
MADE IN MEXICO
XXL

ST EVANS
XXL
100% COTTON
RN 88040
MADE IN HAITI

Caribbean Dream
-L-
100% COTTON

BROCKUM WORLDWIDE
MADE IN U.S.A.
XL
CARE/CONTENT OVER

Q-TEES®
of California
L
MADE IN U.S.A.

MY SHIRT IS MADE IN THE U.S.A.
L 42-44

Sportswear
50% POLYESTER
50% COTTON
MACHINE WASH IN
LUKEWARM WATER
DO NOT BLEACH
TUMBLE DRY, WARM
MADE IN U.S.A.
RN 83961
MEDIUM

STAR PRINTS
MADE IN U.S.A.

JERZEES
100% COMBED COTTON
L
MADE IN U.S.A.

XL

L (42-44)
Healthknit

SOFTEE
MADE IN U.S.A. BY
TeeJays s
CARE AND CONTENT ON REVERSE
L

JERZEES
XL
MADE IN U.S.A.
FOR CARE & CONTENT SEE REVERSE

adidas

ROCK
1776 Broadway New York, NY 10019

GILDAN
ULTRA COTTON
XL

XL
SUPER STITCH INC, dba
STORMIN' NORMAN

Murina®

TULTEX
COTTON
PRESHRUNK

TAILORED BY
Pitt Bro
INC. BRONX, 58, N.Y.

M 38-40
le brève

SOFFE SHIRTS
50% COMBED COTTON

Rap Tees:

A Collection of Hip-Hop T-Shirts 1980–1999

By DJ Ross One

 powerHouse Books

Brooklyn, New York

INTRODUCTION
By Ross Schwartzman AKA DJ Ross One

The hip-hop t-shirt has always been a rare, even mysterious item. While rap albums were on the shelves of record stores across the country, the corresponding shirts were primarily sold in limited numbers at concerts or given away as promotional items, making them sacred objects for collectors of rap memorabilia. Such scarcity has placed the hip-hop t-shirt in a unique position. On the one hand, its elusive nature has generated a great deal of interest from a small community of collectors in the digital era, with bidding wars generating hundreds of dollars. On the other hand, there has been little attention paid to the kind of innovative design so many of these t-shirts display. You are far more likely to see a new shirt that borrows imagery from a vintage rap tee than you are to ever see the original that inspired it. Born from this strange combination of fervor and obscurity, *Rap Tees* is an attempt to satisfy both the most obsessive collector and those simply interested in hip-hop's contribution to design,

contemporary branding, and the world of fashion.

This book is also an homage to the ways that classic hip-hop asked its fans to work for inclusion. Whether searching for rare records to sample or paying close attention to wordplay and allusion, rap demanded that its listeners actively engage or forever be left outside its realm. This is no less true of the hip-hop t-shirt, and their lasting appeal may be linked to how they signify one's commitment to the music. To put on a hip-hop t-shirt in the 80s and 90s was to announce that you had done enough work to receive a shirt. To wear one was to proclaim, in the spirit of KRS-One, "I am hip-hop." And for a young listener like myself growing up in the suburbs of Ohio, earning the right to say such a thing was no small feat.

I bought my first rap tee in 1992. It was a black Beastie Boys shirt with an outtake image from Glen E. Friedman's *Check Your Head* photo session spread across the chest (262). In the photo, MCA is wearing a Champion hoodie, baggy jeans, and a knit

hat. That t-shirt instantly became both part of my wardrobe and an inspiration for it. Around the same time, I got my first Public Enemy shirt through a mail-order form found in the *Apocalypse '91: The Enemy Strikes Black* CD insert (103). Unlike the Beastie Boys shirt, there was no photo, just a simple but bold design. On the front, the word "Enemy" blazes across the chest in athletic script, while on the back Chuck D's iconic crosshair logo keeps watch. Its aesthetic was part sports team, part punk, part militia, and 100% defiant. Wearing it seemed to instantly grant me an informal membership to a revolutionary club. From these two shirts my collection slowly started to grow, each new addition a declaration of my undying fandom. Little did I know that my hunt for hip-hop clothing and ephemera would last the next 20 years.

As the 90s gave way to the 2000s, many early shirts became increasingly scarce. eBay appeared and provided an outlet for my borderline obsessive search. Scouring the Internet proved an efficient way to fill the gaps in my collection, but certain "holy grails" were still impossible to track down. While a coveted De La Soul shirt was no longer an inconceivable find, locating an original Showbiz & A.G. "Soul Clap" sweatshirt would still require a trip to Showbiz's studio in the Bronx with hopes of unearthing his last remaining crewneck from the 1992 video shoot (224). Being a traveling DJ also broadened the scope of my search. I was digging in record and vintage shops across the world and meeting other collectors along the way. In Japan, I met fanatics who shared my obsession and so became both competitors and friends. We waxed poetic in broken English about the shirts still on our want lists, and the trivial but indispensable details that made each one so unique: the subtle differences in hand-drawn graphics, early Screen Stars and Hanes tags, and which 1980s XLs fit more like a modern-day medium than a large (they never actually fit like an XL). I

realized that no single person could ever amass the ultimate collection, but as a collaborative effort the missing pieces could be found. With generous help from DJs, collectors, vintage dealers, old friends, and new friends from around the world, this book is the realization of that ideal, unattainable collection of rap t-shirts.

As the book began to take shape, I reached out to influential graphic designers like Cey Adams and Eric Haze to talk about their shirt and logo designs, which helped forge hip-hop's visual identity. I began to see a lineage in the shirts that mirrored the music. The designers borrowed imagery from the past to create iconic new logos, while rap music was simultaneously on a sampling spree. Even the street-corner bootlegs of the mid 90s (a mishmash of colorful, collaged graphics that seemed like eyesores in 1996) have come to perfectly encapsulate the spirit of that moment in time. Eventually I found myself on the phone with Russell Simmons, both

of us a bit confused as to how we got there, talking about Kurtis Blow, Run DMC, and the creative process behind the earliest hip-hop merchandise. The book loosely flows from Old School, to East Coast (specifically the Golden Era through the late 90s), Miami Bass, Southern Rap, West Coast, and finally hip-hop related films, with a few genre-unspecific shirts sprinkled throughout. After countless hours of digging, editing, and steaming the wrinkles out of crumpled fabric, *Rap Tees* is here to immortalize the shirts of my rap heroes and hopefully provide a unique visual history of hip-hop's greatest era.

001 Sugar Hill Gang
World Tour; 1980

Joe Conzo
Cold Crush Four fans
Harlem World, New York City; 1981

Cathy Campbell
Charlie Ahearn directs the Fantastic 5 in *Wild Style* basketball scene
Bronx; 1981

002   Grandmaster Flash & The Furious 5
"It's Nasty"; 1983

003 Afrika Bambaataa & Soul Sonic Force
"Renegades of Funk"; 1983

004 Enjoy! Records
Japanese bootleg; Late 80s

005   Swatch World Breakdance Championship at The Roxy
1984
Note: Artwork by Keith Haring

006   *New York City Fresh Festival*
1984
Note: Artwork by Keith Haring

The Keith Haring artwork was done through the deal with Swatch. When they signed on, they had him create that artwork. When we created *Fresh Fest* it wasn't just a rap show. It was all about the subculture, which included graffiti, breakdance, and the music. That's what Swatch was buying into. Keith Haring was very popular, but also very early in his career at that point. It was brilliant for him, he later got to design watches with Swatch, and got a ton of exposure. *Fresh Fest* really opened the eyes of a lot of the big advertisers who then started to pay attention and jump on the bandwagon. They could see hip-hop becoming a direct pipeline to that new young energy.

At the time we were making these shirts more for marketing, and the merchandising side was all new to us. We believed in the value of what we were doing, and we knew this was the biggest newest thing, but we didn't make big money from the merchandising. Nothing like what happens today.
— Cedric Walker, founder of the *Fresh Festival*

The *Fresh Fest* was the light that lead to the way we brand hip-hop today. Collaborations with clothing lines, headphones, sneakers—it all started there.

I remember being 13 and I was a dancer on the tour. I had on a *Fresh Fest* shirt walking into the venue, and this grown white lady with huge boobs was like, "Can I please have that shirt?" Then she took off her shirt showing me her boobs and waited 'til I gave it to her. That was the highlight of me becoming a teen.
— Jermaine Dupri, founder of So So Def Recordings as well as *Fresh Festival* dancer/performer

New York City Fresh Festival
1984
Note: The *New York City Fresh Festival* was the first large-scale hip-hop tour.

008 *New York City Fresh Festival II*
1985
Note: Design by Cey Adams

I was making this shirt (008) while trying to come up with a logo for Run DMC. It's a knock-off of the Frankie Goes to Hollywood "Relax" shirt. The letters aren't perfectly lined up because I had to do them with a ruler, a t-square, and a copy machine. — Cey Adams, RUSH Productions/Def Jam creative director, 1983–99

009 *New York City Fresh Festival II*
1985
Note: Design by Cey Adams

010   Whodini / *Fresh Festival Tour*
1985
Note: Glows in the dark, design by Cey Adams

011   Kurtis Blow / *Fresh Festival Tour*
1985
This was all done by hand. It was the ugliest shirt. Kurtis hated
this. He thought the light blue was so soft. — Cey Adams

012   *New York City Fresh Festival III Tour*
1986

013   *Jam-A-Tron Street Festival*
      Atlanta; 1985

014   Grandmaster Flash
      1987
      Opposite Page

015 Kurtis Blow
"King of Rap"; 1985

We were artist development people. Every logo and tagline was very important to us. When I first named Kurtis Blow the "King of Rap" and put his picture on the 12" cover for "The Breaks," he actually became the King of Rap, simply by us calling him that. That was the first time people had seen a rap artist ever. When you heard the name Kurtis Blow you already knew what he looked like. It was the start of the branding process. We fought and worked for that because we were the only people young enough to believe that these hip-hop artists were part of a cultural movement. They were making a statement that was more lasting and stable than the piece of vinyl that they came out on. — Russell Simmons, founder of RUSH Productions and cofounder of Def Jam

016 Whodini
1986

017 Whodini
Back in Black; 1986

018 UTFO
Lethal; 1987

019 UTFO
Skeezer Pleezer; 1986

020 Fat Boys
Mid 80s

021 Fat Boys
The Fat Boys Are Back; 1985

022 Heavy D. & the Boyz
Living Large; 1987

023   Kool Moe Dee
How Ya Like Me Now, 1987

024   Kool Moe Dee
1988

025   Kool Moe Dee
1986

Ricky Powell
Rev Run & Mike D
Hollis, Queens; 1987

Several of the clubs and record pools had jackets. The Disco Fever, and the S.U.R.E. Record Pool for DJs. Usually they were satin. I thought the Def Jam jacket would look better in wool. More like a varsity jacket. We embroidered the logo on the back, and the tone arm with personalized names on the front. Even though there was a huge demand for them we never sold them. Only artists and crew had them. — Rick Rubin, cofounder of Def Jam

026 **Def Jam**
Jacket; 1985
Note: Courtesy of Bill "Ill Badler" Adler

Rick Rubin produced the very first run of Def Jam jackets, which were maroon. They went to Rick and Russ, the Beasties, L.L., Burzootie, and very few others. Maybe there were a dozen made altogether. Then this run, in black, came out. That's when Lyor Cohen, Heidi Smith, and I were finally blessed. It was the year of our lord 1985. — Bill Adler, publicity director at Def Jam 1984–90

027 **Def Jam**
Varsity jacket; Late 80s
Note: Courtesy of Janette Beckman

I was always around the Def Jam office on Elizabeth Street and one day it was either Bill (Adler) or Lyor said to me, "Do you want a jacket?" It had my name on it and it was just the coolest thing. I wore it every single day, I was thrilled.
— Janette Beckman, photographer

The promotional item that bestowed the most status on those who wore it was without question the Def Jam jacket. It was the first and the best piece of hip-hop label promo clothing. It was issued only to limited staff members during their heyday. It was the first time we experienced the feeling of "Holy shit. Who's that? Where do I get that jacket? Who is that guy? He must be somebody important."
— Jonathan "Shecky Green" Shecter, founding editor of *The Source* magazine

028   Def Jam
1985

029   Def Jam
Artist roster; Late 80s

030 Def Jam
Tonearm logo; Late 80s

031 RUSH Productions
Artist roster; Mid 80s
Note: RUSH Productions was the management and promotion company of Russell "Rush" Simmons.

Glen E. Friedman
Run DMC
Santa Monica Pier; 1985

The Run DMC logo came about when I was asked by Ashley Newton at 4th & B'way to design a 12" promo sleeve for the first UK release of "My Adidas." I was an in-house designer at Island Records. We would often have to design the sleeve then and there, so the logo was an immediate response to the music. Ashley's brief was for the sleeve art to "Grab attention and hit hard, make the sleeve look as raw, tough, and punchy as the music."

Promos were often limited to two colors and no photography so I came up with this strong graphic solution. We had a limited number of fonts at our disposal and the Franklin Gothic font by MF Benton was in our armory. It's forthright and unfaddish. With the two sets of three letters it came together really well and we printed the sleeve red and black with the name reversed out in the white of the card.

It was always a thrill to see people wearing it at the time of release and now with all the variations and look-alikes it's still fresh. The best thing for a designer is to see a piece of work do what it is intended to do and stand the test of time.
— Stephanie Nash, art director, Island Records

That logo came from London. We went there for the first time, saw that logo, that someone made in the British office, took that shit and ran with it. The greatest logo that hip-hop has today, still. The most used, the most bought, sold, the most resold.
— Russell Simmons

I remain surprised and flattered that this logo is loved by so many. Shocked really. I think artists like Lil Wayne and Rihanna wearing it has introduced the logo to a new generation.
— Rev Run, Run DMC

032   Run DMC
1986

033　Run DMC
King of Rock; 1985

034　Run DMC
"Hit It Run"; 1986

035　Run DMC
Raising Hell; 1986

036   Run DMC
Raising Hell tour bootleg; 1986

037   Run DMC
Tougher Than Leather; 1987

038   Run DMC
Tougher Than Leather tour; 1988

039 Run DMC
Raising Hell; 1986

040 Run DMC
Raising Hell; 1986

041 Run DMC
Raising Hell; 1986

042 Run DMC
Tougher Than Leather / "Run's House" World Tour, 1988
Note: "Run's House" logo by Cey Adams

043 Run DMC
Tougher Than Leather, 1988

044 Run DMC
Tougher Than Leather / "Run's House", 1988

045 Run DMC
Bootleg; Mid 80s

Selling bootlegs was just a way for people to make money outside of the concert. When we were on tour we used to take a lot of the bootlegs after the shows. We'd go outside of the show with tour security and just jack them. In retrospect I wish I would have kept more, because it was one of the only ways you could see who all was on the bill. — Cey Adams

046 Run DMC
Raising Hell tour bootleg; 1986

047   Run DMC
Raising Hell tour bootleg; 1986

048   Run DMC
Tour bootleg; Late 80s

049   Run DMC
Tougher Than Leather tour bootleg; 1988

050 Run DMC / Adidas
"My Adidas" sweatshirt. Mid 80s

051   Run DMC / Adidas
"My Adidas" sweatshirt; Mid 80s

052   Run DMC / Adidas
"Kings from Queens" sweatshirt; Mid 80s

053   Run DMC / Adidas
"Hollis Crew" sweatshirt; Mid 80s

054   Run DMC / Adidas
Mid 80s

055   Run DMC / Adidas
"My Adidas"; Mid 80s

056   Run DMC / Adidas
"Kings from Queens"; Mid 80s

057   Run DMC / Adidas
"Hollis Crew"; Mid 80s

058   Run DMC / Adidas
Fly Boys sweatshirt; Mid 80s
Note: Unreleased reversible sweatshirt sample

059 **Beastie Boys**
1986
Note: Never officially released

Back then people were pretty homophobic, and [the Beastie Boys] were the least homophobic of the people who walked the planet. Definitely the least homophobic of all the rappers. There's nothing good about [the shirt], but all they wanted to do was piss people off. That's all that was about. — Russell Simmons

060   **Beastie Boys**
Get Busy or Get Lost!; 1987
Note: Front logo design by Cey Adams

The Beasties commissioned me to do that in logo in 1983. Later we revised it in 1986. I made 35 dollars for that logo. It's their favorite logo to this day. — Cey Adams

I got this shirt straight from [the Beastie Boys]. You couldn't get one, and I remember thinking, "Holy shit, there's a shirt that says Get Off My Dick." It was just next level. Before that time, we were hanging out at nightclubs all over the world where normally you'd kinda have to dress up. Then came 1985–86, you could roll up in a baseball hat, jeans, Ewings, and a shirt that says "Get Off My Dick," and you're up in the club! This was pre-Naomi Cambpell, pre-bottle service. You're just in the club full of models and rich people, and I'm basically a 17- or 18-year-old complete dirtbag that's into hip-hop and punk rock and skateboarding. It was kinda mind blowing.
— Paul Mittleman, Stussy creative director, 1997–2011

[Def Jam] always believed in artist development. The other labels thought these were disposable artists. We knew that they were cultural, career artists that needed longterm branding and longterm thinking. The stuff we wrote on the back of the Beastie Boys t-shirts, the ideas, we were very thoughtful. They really didn't have a sense of who they were in the rap world, they were just punk rockers who loved rap music. They didn't realize that they could dress like the punk rockers they were, and be rappers. They didn't know that, so we had to make them know that.
— Russell Simmons

The roadies loved these, but people were complaining so they did the censored version (064). I was like, you know what you might as well not even do it! — Cey Adams

062   Beastie Boys
Get Off My Dick; 1986

063   Beastie Boys
Get Off My Dick; 1986

064   Beastie Boys
Get Off My ****; 1986

065 Beastie Boys
1987
Note: Courtesy of Eric Haze

I designed the original (diamond) Beastie Boys logo and it was based on the iconic Harley Davidson logo. We all wore and cared about t-shirt culture before there was such a thing. Cool band t-shirts, cool hot rod t-shirts, cool school shirts, cool surf shirts. We were obsessed. — Rick Rubin

066 Beastie Boys
"Fight For Your Right (To Party!)"; 1987

067 Beastie Boys
"Fight For Your Right (To Party!)"; 1987
Note: Spraypainted back graphic by Cey Adams

068 Beastie Boys
Licensed to Ill bootleg; 1987

069 Beastie Boys
Licensed to Ill tour;1987
Note: *Licensed to Ill* 1987 tour graphic design by Eric Haze

070 Beastie Boys
Licensed to Ill U.K. tour; 1987

071   Beastie Boys
Licensed to Ill tour bootleg; 1987

072   Beastie Boys
Licensed to Ill tour; 1987

073   Beastie Boys
"Time to Get Ill" bootleg; Late 80s

074   Beastie Boys
"Kickin' It Live" Local Crew; 1987

075   Run DMC & Beastie Boys
Licensed To Ill tour bootleg; 1987

076   Run DMC & Beastie Boys
Together Forever tour; 1987

077 **Run DMC & Beastie Boys**
Together Forever tour; 1987
Note: Design by Cey Adams; Photo by Lynn Goldsmith

078 **Run DMC & Beastie Boys**
Together Forever tour; 1987
Note: Original shrinkwrapped packaging

Janette Beckman
Eric B. & Rakim
New York City; 1987

079   *Def Jam 87* Tour
1987
Note: *Def Jam 87* logo design by Eric Haze

080   *Def Jam 87* Tour
1987

081   Def Jam / L.L. Cool J
Bigger And Deffer tour, Local Crew; 1987

082   Def Jam / L.L. Cool J
Bigger And Deffer tour bootleg; 1987

083 L.L. Cool J
Radio; 1985

084 L.L. Cool J
1986

085　L.L. Cool J
Radio bootleg; Mid 80s

086　L.L. Cool J
1986

087　L.L. Cool J
Bigger And Deffer bootleg; Late 80s

088　L.L. Cool J
Bigger And Deffer bootleg sweatshirt; Late 80s

089　L.L. Cool J
Bigger And Deffer long sleeve shirt; 1987
Note: Logo design by Eric Haze

090　L.L. Cool J
Troop warm-up suit; Late 80s

Ricky Powell
L.L. Cool J with Cut Creator and E-Love
Los Angeles; 1988

091   L.L. Cool J
Troop warm-up suit; Late 80s

I was out on the road with the bands, and I was using local copy shops in whatever city we were in. The merchandiser was always on tour as well, so I'd be doing stuff in my hotel room at times. That's why it was all kind of cut and paste, because I'd just lay something down with clear tape on a t-shirt and explain to the guy, "This is the size I want it to be." Sometimes they got it right, sometimes they didn't. We were changing designs mid-tour, and if something sold out they would just say, "We need another design." Also I had instant access to the bands, so if I did something I could show it to them right away to get their opinion. I had to always explain what the colorways were because you couldn't show it in color, so I'd lay it out in black and white along with Pantone swatches to give an idea. We were all friends, so if they didn't like a design, I wasn't gonna try to force it down their throats. — Cey Adams

L.L. Cool J
"Nitro" World Tour, 1989–90
Note: Design by Cey Adams

093   L.L. Cool J
"Nitro" tour; 1989–90

094   L.L. Cool J
"Nitro" tour; 1989–90

095   L.L. Cool J
Tour bootleg; Late 80s

096 L.L. Cool J
Mama Said Knock You Out; 1990

097 L.L. Cool J
1991

Looking at these shirts makes me feel like I'm in a museum looking at a hip-hop art exhibit. It really does represent the cultural phenomenon of the rap and hip-hop scene in the 80s that paved the way for today's hip-hop music. It is truly a piece of history.
— L.L. Cool J

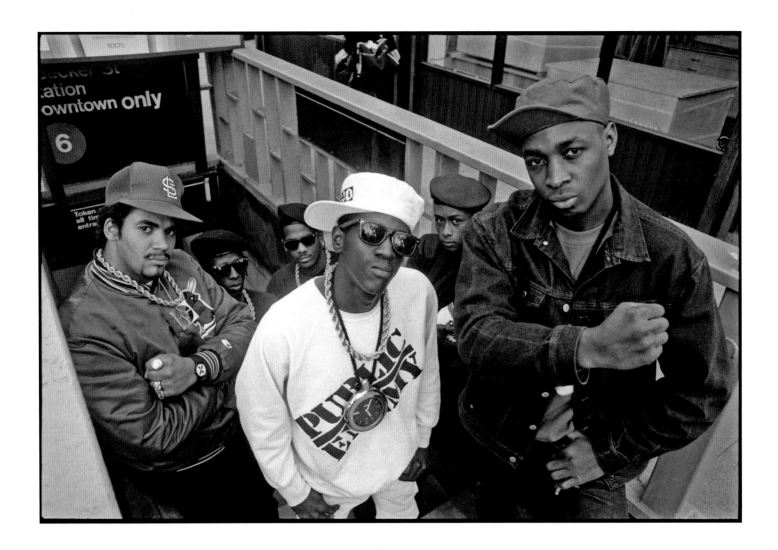

Glen E. Friedman
Public Enemy
New York City; 1988

Chuck had the vision for the logo and uniforms. I think that's part of what motivated him to make music at all. He saw the whole thing from the beginning. The music was just a piece. — Rick Rubin

098 **Public Enemy**
1988
Note: Crosshair logo design by Chuck D

Public Enemy's shirt with the military stencil-style logo is my all time favorite. Classic black and white, bold and timeless, could be a punk band, rock group, whatever. Doesn't really say "hip-hop" but P.E. was so much more than a hip-hop group.
— Stretch Armstrong

099   Public Enemy
1988

100   Public Enemy
1988

101   Public Enemy
Late 80s

Public Enemy
It Takes a Nation of Millions to Hold Us Back; 1988

The Public Enemy shirts were ALL per Chuck's instructions. Nobody takes credit for designing P.E. shirts because Chuck played such an important role in the design. He was really hands on, so we didn't take as much creative license. — Cey Adams

103   Public Enemy
1991

104   Public Enemy
Baseball jersey; 1991

105   Public Enemy
Bootleg; Early 90s

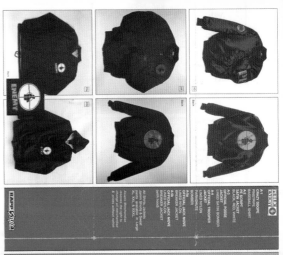

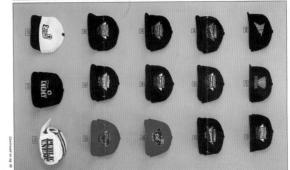

1-800 955-PEGEAR
or 1-800 955-7343
1-516 489-4700

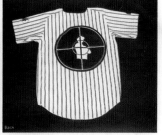

  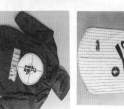

106 Public Enemy
Yo! Bum Rush the Show bootleg; Late 80s

107 Public Enemy
Asiatic Merch. / Rapp Style order forms; Early 90s
Previous Spread

108 Public Enemy
It Takes a Nation of Millions... bootleg; Late 80s

109 Public Enemy
"911 Is a Joke" bootleg; Early 90s

110 Public Enemy
"Fight the Power" Live! bootleg; Early 90s

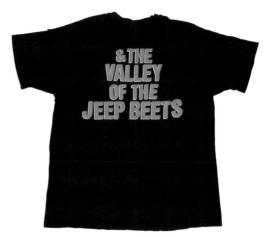

111   Public Enemy
"Black Steel In the Hour of Chaos" bootleg; 1989

112   Terminator X
Terminator X & the Valley of the Jeep Beats; 1991

113 Public Enemy
"Welcome to the Terror Dome"; 1990

114 Public Enemy
"Welcome to the Terrordome"; 1990

115 Public Enemy
Fear of a Black Planet; 1990

116   Public Enemy
Apocalypse '91 The Enemy Strikes Black; 1991

117   Public Enemy
Apocalypse 91... The Enemy Strikes Black; 1991

118   Public Enemy
Early 90s

119   Public Enemy
1993

120   Public Enemy
Baseball jersey; 1993

121   Public Enemy
Jacket; 1993

122 Public Enemy
Early 90s

123 Public Enemy
Early 90s

124 Public Enemy
"Give It Up";1994

125 *Bring the Noise* Tour
Bootleg; 1988

126 *Bring the Noise* Tour
Bootleg; 1988
Opposite Page

I remember being at the Spectrum for this. It was a huge, epic Public Enemy show. In fact, Chuck D later told me that it was the greatest hip-hop concert of all time. It was a combination of the lineup, and that it happened right at the moment when "Rebel Without a Pause" came out. That song was a game changer of titanic proportions—a paradigm shift. The concert was perfectly timed to their hottest moment, with that record being so huge. — Jonathan "Shecky Green" Shecter

127   Eric B. & Rakim
Paid In Full; 1988
Note: Design by Cey Adams

128   Eric B. & Rakim
Follow the Leader tour jacket; 1988–89
Note: Courtesy of Bill Adler

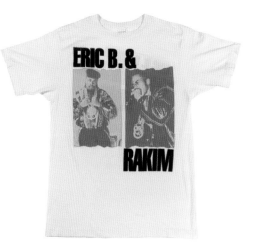

129   Eric B. & Rakim
Paid In Full; 1987

130   Eric B. & Rakim
"Ain't No Joke"; 1988

131   Eric B. & Rakim
Let the Rhythm Hit 'Em; 1990

132 Eric B. & Rakim
Let the Rhythm Hit 'Em; 1990

133 Eric B. & Rakim
Let the Rhythm Hit 'Em promo; 1990

134   Big Daddy Kane
Long Live the Kane promo; 1988

135   Big Daddy Kane
It's a Big Daddy Thing; 1989

136   Big Daddy Kane
"Pimpin Ain't Easy"; 1990

137   Biz Markie
The Diabolical Biz Markie promo; 1989

138   Biz Markie
The Diabolical Biz Markie; 1989

139   Cold Chillin'
Bootleg; Early 90s
Note: Cold Chillin' logo design by Eric Haze

140   Cold Chillin' Records
Where the Music Is Hot; Late 80s

141   DJ Jazzy Jeff
    "Parents Just Don't Understand" bootleg; 1988

Man... I remember getting these shirts for the "Run's House" Tour and saying "We Made it... Our shirts are next to Run DMC and Public Enemy." — DJ Jazzy Jeff

142   DJ Jazzy Jeff & The Fresh Prince
    Tour; 1988
    Note: Design by Cey Adams

143 DJ Jazzy Jeff & The Fresh Prince
"Girls Ain't Nothing But Trouble"; 1988

144 DJ Jazzy Jeff & The Fresh Prince
He's the DJ... I'm the Rapper promo; 1988

145 DJ Jazzy Jeff & The Fresh Prince
"Summertime" promo tank top; 1991

146 Slick Rick
The Great Adventures of Slick Rick; 1989

147 Slick Rick
The Great Adventures of Slick Rick, 1989

148 **EPMD**
Strictly Business bootleg sweatshirt; 1988

Nothing symbolized the look of hip-hop more than the Run DMC logo, so the EPMD logo was my first real stab at taking that new hip-hop look and seeing how far I could push it. I designed the original EPMD logo from scratch, by hand, with no typesetting. Just rapidograph and a t-square. — Eric Haze, artist and graphic designer

149 EPMD
Strictly Business; 1988

150 EPMD
Unfinished Business; 1989

151 EPMD
Business As Usual; 1990

152   EPMD
Bootleg; Late 80s

153   EPMD
Unfinished Business; 1989

154   Hit Squad
Artist roster; Early 90s

155   EPMD
"Crossover" promo; 1992

Break from the Pack • Join the Sleeping Bag/Fresh Team

● Style #424
Parachute Silk
SLEEPING BAG
colors: Blk, Blue
● Style #724 Raglan
Parachute Silk
FRESH RECORDS
colors: Blue Only
All jackets are lined
and have an inside
pocket $125.00

● Style #428 Wool/
Leather Bomber Style.
All jackets are quilt
lined and have inside
pockets. Outstanding
in its field!
SLEEPING BAG
colors: Yellow/Blk,
Grn/Blk, Purple/Blk
$175.00
● Denim Jackets are
stone and acid
washed for additional
faded look. SLEEPING
BAG or FRESH logo
available in various
colors. Includes
patches $95.00

● Designer Vests come in leather and canvas. Double lock
frontier pocket. All have cartoon lining. SLEEPING BAG
colors only: Blk, Red, Yellow $95.00

● Heavy Duty Sweats are the Defest. 100% cotton.
SLEEPING BAG Blk/Pk, Pk/Blk, FRESH Blk/Blue,
Blue/Wht. T-shirts are 100% cotton and come in FRESH
Blue and SLEEPING BAG Yellow. Sweats $35.00 T-shirts $10.00

● Fanny Pack is 100%
cotton canvas
Blk/Yellow only
$20.00

Special Thanks to
Evan, Nancy, Nicol,
Missy and Mai. All
logos (except T-shirts)
100% cotton embroi-
dered. All colors not
shown. Actual colors
may vary slightly.
Comes in sizes M, L,
XL. Cannot be bought
in stores.

ORDER FORM

ITEM	COLOR	SIZE	QTY	ITEM PRICE	TOTAL PRICE

Please make check or
money order payable to:
SLEEPING BAG/FRESH RECORDS
1974 Broadway
New York, NY 10023

Total order	
NY Residents add applicable sales tax	
$7.50 shipping charge	
GRAND TOTAL	

NAME
ADDRESS   Apt.
CITY
STATE   ZIP
Prices as of: June 1, 1989

☐ Check ☐ Money Order ☐ MasterCard ☐ VISA

Charge Card Number:

Issuing Bank

Expiration Date   Signature

Please allow 4-6 weeks for delivery.

156   Sleeping Bag / Fresh Records 12" Insert Order Form
Late 80s

157   Sleeping Bag Records
Varsity jacket; Late 80s

158 Heavy D. & The Boyz
Big Tyme varsity jacket; 1989
Note: Personalized "The Hevster"

159 Payday
Varsity jacket; Late 80s
Note: Courtesy of Eric Haze, designer of the logo. Payday was originally a NYC hip hop club that grew into a label, known for briefly signing a young Jay Z.

160 Profile Records
Varsity jacket; Late 80s

161   Boogie Down Productions
By All Means Necessary; 1988

162   Boogie Down Productions & Big Daddy Kane
Concert; 1988

163   Boogie Down Productions
"Love's Gonna Get'Cha"; 1990

164   Boogie Down Productions
Sex & Violence promo hoodie; 1992

165   The Stop the Violence Movement
1989
Note: Produced by 4 Star General, London

166   Boogie Down Productions
      "Stop the Violence"; 1988

167   Boogie Down Productions
      Ghetto Music; 1989

168   Boogie Down Productions
      Ghetto Music: The Blueprint of Hip Hop; 1989

169 X-Clan
Xodus; 1992

170 X-Clan
Early 90s

171 X-Clan
Xodus; 1992

172 X-Clan
Early 90s

173　Universal Zulu Nation
Early 90s

UNIVERSAL ZULU NATION

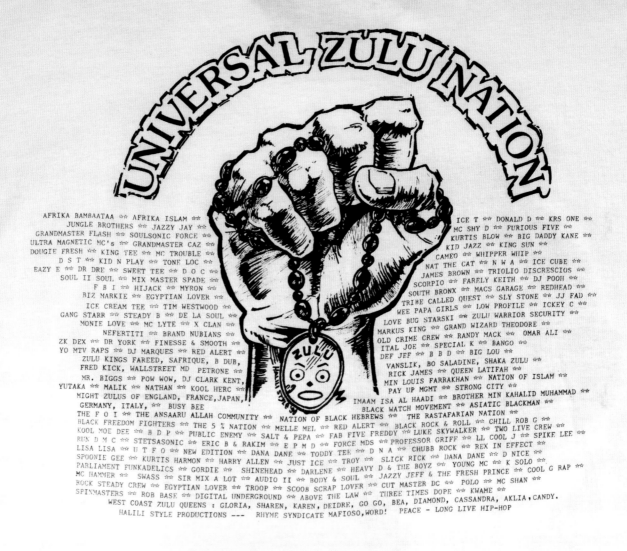

AFRIKA BAMBAATAA *** AFRIKA ISLAM ***
JUNGLE BROTHERS *** JAZZY JAY ***
GRANDMASTER FLASH *** SOULSONIC FORCE ***
ULTRA MAGNETIC MC's *** GRANDMASTER CAZ ***
DOUGIE FRESH *** KING TEE *** MC TROUBLE ***
D S T *** KID N PLAY *** TONE LOC ***
EAZY E *** DR DRE *** SWEET TEE *** D O C ***
SOUL II SOUL *** MIX MASTER SPADE ***
F B I *** HIJACK *** MYRON ***
BIZ MARKIE *** EGYPTIAN LOVER ***
ICE CREAM TEE *** TIM WESTWOOD ***
GANG STARR *** STEADY B *** DE LA SOUL ***
MONIE LOVE *** MC LYTE *** X CLAN ***
NEFERTITI *** BRAND NUBIANS ***
ZK DEX *** DR YORK *** FINESSE & SMOOTH ***
YO MTV RAPS *** DJ MARQUES *** RED ALERT ***
ZULU KINGS FAREED, SAFRIQUE, B DUB,
FRED KICK, WALLSTREET MD PETRONE
MR. BIGGS *** POW WOW, DJ CLARK KENT,
YUTAKA *** MALIK *** NATHAN *** KOOL HERC ***
MIGHT ZULUS OF ENGLAND, FRANCE, JAPAN,
GERMANY, ITALY, *** BUSY BEE
THE F O I *** THE ANSAARU ALLAH COMMUNITY *** NATION OF BLACK HEBREWS ***

ICE T *** DONALD D *** KRS ONE ***
MC SHY D *** FURIOUS FIVE ***
KURTIS BLOW *** BIG DADDY KANE ***
KID JAZZ *** KING SUN ***
CAMEO *** WHIPPER WHIP ***
NAT THE CAT *** N W A *** ICE CUBE ***
JAMES BROWN *** TRIOLIO DISCRESCIOS ***
SCORPIO *** FARELY KEITH *** DJ POOH ***
SOUTH BRONX *** MACS GARAGE *** REDHEAD ***
TRIBE CALLED QUEST *** SLY STONE *** JJ FAD ***
WEE PAPA GIRLS *** LOW PROFILE *** ICKEY C ***
LOVE BUG STARSKI *** ZULU WARRIOR SECURITY ***
MARKUS KING *** GRAND WIZARD THEODORE ***
OLD CRIME CREW *** RANDY MACK *** OMAR ALI ***
ITAL JOE *** SPECIAL K *** BANGO ***
DEF JEF *** B B D *** BIG LOU ***
VANSLIK, BO SALADINE, SHAKA ZULU ***
RICK JAMES *** QUEEN LATIFAH ***
MIN LOUIS FARRAKHAN *** NATION OF ISLAM ***
PAY UP MGMT *** STRONG CITY ***
IMAAM ISA AL HAADI *** BROTHER MIN KAHALID MUHAMMAD ***
BLACK WATCH MOVEMENT *** ASIATIC BLACKMAN ***
THE RASTAFARIAN NATION ***

BLACK FREEDOM FIGHTERS *** THE 5 % NATION *** MELLE MEL *** RED ALERT *** BLACK ROCK & ROLL *** CHILL ROB G ***
KOOL MOE DEE *** B D P *** PUBLIC ENEMY *** SALT & PEPA *** FAB FIVE FREDDY *** LUKE SKYWALKER *** TWO LIVE CREW ***
RUN D M C *** STETSASONIC *** ERIC B & RAKIM *** E P M D *** FORCE MDS *** PROFESSOR GRIFF *** LL COOL J *** SPIKE LEE
LISA LISA *** U T F O *** NEW EDITION *** DANA DANE *** TODDY TEE *** D N A *** CHUBB ROCK *** REX IN EFFECT ***
SPOONIE GEE *** KURTIS HARMON *** HARRY ALLEN *** JUST ICE *** TROY *** SLICK RICK *** DANA DANE *** D NICE ***
PARLIAMENT FUNKADELICS *** GORDIE *** SHINEHEAD *** DARLENE *** HEAVY D & THE BOYZ *** YOUNG MC *** K SOLO ***
MC HAMMER *** SWASS *** SIR MIX A LOT *** AUDIO II *** BODY & SOUL *** JAZZY JEFF & THE FRESH PRINCE *** COOL G RAP ***
ROCK STEADY CREW *** EGYPTIAN LOVER *** TROOP *** SCOOB SCRAP LOVER *** CUT MASTER DC *** POLO *** MC SHAN ***
SPINMASTERS *** ROB BASE *** DIGITAL UNDERGROUND *** ABOVE THE LAW *** THREE TIMES DOPE *** KWAME ***
WEST COAST ZULU QUEENS : GLORIA, SHAREN, KAREN, DEIDRE, GO GO, BEA, DIAMOND, CASSANDRA, AKLIA, CANDY.
HALILI STYLE PRODUCTIONS --- RHYME SYNDICATE MAFIOSO, WORD! PEACE - LONG LIVE HIP-HOP

174   **DJ Red Alert**
Red Alert Productions varsity jacket; Late 80s

It's funny, when this logo got made they brought me down to the office at Black Ink (the design company) and showed me the options. I always just said "Red Alert Productions," and I never even realized that the initials spelled R.A.P. When I saw it broken down in that logo, I said, "I must have this one." It was a lucky surprise, a blessing. I probably made 25 jackets, all to be given away as promo. At that time you were trying anything to get your name out there and be recognized. — DJ Red Alert

175   DJ Red Alert
Red Alert Productions hoodie; Late 80s
Note: Produced by 4 Star General, London

176   98.7 Kiss FM NYC
Promo; Late 80s

177   98.7 Kiss FM NYC
Born to Be Hot promo; Late 80s

178   107.5 FM WBLS
My Number promo; Late 80s

179 Stetsasonic
In Full Gear promo; 1988

180 Jungle Brothers
Safari 4 Survival Japan tour; 1989

181   Jungle Brothers
World tour; 1989

182   De La Soul
"Me Myself & I" bootleg; Late 80s

The Native Tongues were coming up with creative ideas about how they wanted to project themselves with fashion, colors, and overall awareness. They had seen what BDP and Public Enemy were bringing to the table and took it to another level, with a more Afrocentric awareness. — DJ Red Alert

183 De La Soul
1989
Note: Logo design by Cey Adams

We were always interested in not only flipping and trying different images but also trying different styles with our logo. If you notice, nearly every other rap group maintains their same logo from day one. We always wanted to change things up as much as we could, especially when it came to shirt ideas. — Posdnuos, De La Soul

184 De La Soul
3 Feet High and Rising; 1989
Note: Design by Michael Uman and Cey Adams

185   De La Soul
This is My De La Soul T-shirt; 1989
Note: Design by Michael Uman and Cey Adams

186   De La Soul
3 Feet High and Rising Europe tour; 1989

187   De La Soul
Is Dead; 1991
Note: Design by Mark Weinberg

188   De La Soul
Is Dead / De La Day promo; 1991

189   De La Soul
"Saturdays" promo; 1991

190   De La Soul
"I Am I Be" promo; 1993

191 De La Soul
Stakes Is High Japan tour; 1996

192 De La Soul
Stakes Is High / "Keep It Real Right!"; 1996

193 De La Soul
Stakes Is High; 1996

194   A Tribe Called Quest
"Footprints"; 1990

195   A Tribe Called Quest
The Low End Theory; 1991

196   A Tribe Called Quest
"Check the Rhyme" promo; 1991

197 A Tribe Called Quest
1993

198 A Tribe Called Quest
1993

199 A Tribe Called Quest
Midnight Marauders; 1993

200 Black Sheep
A Wolf in Sheep's Clothing world tour; 1992

201 Black Sheep
A Wolf in Sheep's Clothing; 1991

202　Leaders of the New School
A Future Without a Past; 1991

203   Monie Love
On Tour; 1991

204   Queen Latifah
All Hail the Queen; 1989

205   Queen Latifah
Nature of a Sista; 1991

206   Queen Latifah
"U.N.I.T.Y." promo; 1993

207 Salt-N-Pepa
Hot, Cool & Vicious; 1986

208 Salt-N-Pepa
"Whatta Man" bootleg; 1994

209   Salt-N-Pepa
Very Necessary tour; 1994

210   Salt-N-Pepa
A Salt with a Deadly Pepa; 1988

211   MC Lyte
Eyes On This; 1989

212   MC Lyte
Act Like You Know; 1991

213   First Priority Music
Late 80s
Note: First Priority's artists included Audio Two and MC Lyte.

214   MC Lyte
"Ruff Neck"; 1993

Prime Minister Pete Nice
MC Serch and Russell Simmons at the Jack The Rapper Convention
Atlanta; 1989

215   3rd Bass
"Steppin' to the A.M."; 1989

216   3rd Bass
Derelicts of Dialect; 1991

217   3rd Bass
World Unity Tour; 1991

218   KMD
Mr. Hood promo; 1991

I lived around the corner from Russell Simmons' office, so RUSH artists were always in the neighborhood. I had this green BMW 5 series and one day I come outside to find it being towed. I figured the driver of the truck was into hip-hop, so I'm like, "Yo listen, if you put my car down I've got KMD t-shirts, 12"s, and even a brand new Def Jam jacket in the trunk. You can have it." She looked at me and said, "I already towed KRS-One and Jam Master Jay. Everybody tries that shit with me. Once the car is up, it's not comin down." — Prime Minister Pete Nice, 3rd Bass

219   Jack the Rapper
Early 90s
Note: Jack The Rapper was the first hip-hop convention.

220   Jive Records
*The *Word is Rap / *Jive is the Word* promo; 1988

221 Jive Records / BMG
Knowledge is the Best Rap promo; Early 90s.

222 Elektra Records
Hard to the Left Rap promo; Early 90s

223 *Yo! MTV Raps*
Early 90s

224   **Showbiz & A.G.**
"Soul Clap" promo sweatshirt; 1992
Note: Courtesy of Showbiz

225   Pete Rock & C.L. Smooth
"It's Not a Game" promo; 1993

226   Pete Rock & C.L. Smooth
All Souled Out promo; 1991

227   Diamond D. & The Psychotic Neurotics
Stunts, Blunts and Hip Hop promo; 1992

228   Main Source
"Just Hangin Out" promo; 1991

229   Ed O.G. & Da Bulldogs
Life of a Kid in the Ghetto promo; 1991

230   Grand Puba
Reel to Reel promo fishing vest; 1992

I made a Grand Puba fishing vest when the fisherman vest was all the rage. Unfortunately I blew the sizing on it and they ran young so I could never rock mine. What a bummer. It was a great idea, but bad execution. — Dante Ross, vice president of A&R, Elektra Records, 1988–96

231   Grand Puba
Early 90s

232   Brand Nubian
"Peace to the Gods"; 1993

233   Gang Starr
Step in the Arena promo; 1991

234   Gang Starr
Step in the Arena promo; 1991

235 Gang Starr
"Mass Appeal" bootleg; 1994

236 Gang Starr
Hard to Earn; 1994

237 Empire Artist Management
Artist roster promo; Mid 90s

238 Gang Starr
Full Clip: A Decade of Gang Starr promo; 1999

239 Jeru The Damaja
The Sun Rises in the East promo; 1994

240 Jeru The Damaja
Wrath of the Math promo; 1996

241   Black Moon
      "I Got Cha Opin" promo; 1994

242   Black Moon
      "I Got Cha Opin" promo; 1994

243   Black Moon
      "I Got Cha Opin" bootleg; 1994

244   Smif-N-Wessun
"Bucktown" bootleg; 1995

245   Das EFX
"Backnaffek"; 1993

246   Das EFX
Hold it Down promo; 1995

247 Masta Ace Incorporated
Sittin' On Chrome football jersey; 1995

The football jersey-as-promo was kinda rare. It was sort of Masta Ace's thing. I got the *Sittin' on Chrome* jersey in '94 from the publicist at Delicious Vinyl. There was actually a typo—it says "Sititin' on Chrome." I think they had to re-run them. — Brent Rollins, designer and creative director

248 Naughty By Nature
"O.P.P." bootleg; 1991

249 Naughty By Nature
"O.P.P."; 1991
Note: Naughty By Nature logo by Mark Weinberg

250 Naughty By Nature
"It's a Kitten Hittin' Day"; 1993

251 Naughty By Nature
19 Naughty III baseball jersey; 1993

252 Naughty By Nature
Janet Jackson bootleg sweatshirt; 1993

253 Naughty By Nature
"It's On" bootleg; 1993

TOMMY BOY

AND WE MAKE GOOD RECORDS, TOO

One piece of hip-hop promo that I always specifically loved was the brown Carhartt Tommy Boy Staff jacket.
— Posdnuos, De La Soul

In the midst of the rap promo t-shirt madness Tommy Boy created a Carhartt jacket with Stussy that was the first link between streetwear and a record label. To me, it was the greatest single piece of promo ever made by anyone. I was always inspired by Tommy Boy.
— Dante Ross

It wasn't merch. It wasn't sold, or if it was they were sold in a very small quantity. It was more of a friends and family thing. It's kind of a mythological object.
— Paul Mittleman

I was lucky to be one of the recipients of the first batch of these. Albee Ragusa, who worked for Tommy Boy at the time, had a great sense of what was hip and he knew how to pick the next big thing. It was the first time a branded piece of apparel was attached to a hip-hop label. I remember the material was super stiff even back in 1992, and it still is. The Def Jam jacket was the coolest, but by this time Def Jam had lost its sheen a little bit, and the Tommy Boy Carhartt actually looked cool as a piece of fashion.
— Jonathan "Shecky Green" Shecter

255   Tommy Boy / Stussy / Carhartt
Staff jacket; Early 90s

256 Beastie Boys
Dusted Elephant; 1992
Note: Artwork by Todd James (REAS)

257 Beastie Boys
The Fat Shit In '92; 1992

258 Beastie Boys
"The Maestro (Fuck All Y'all)"; 1992

259   **Beastie Boys**
Check Your Head; 1992
Note: Photo by Glen E. Friedman, lettering by Eric Haze

260   **Beastie Boys**
Brooklyn Dust Music / *Check Your Head*; 1992
Note: Photo by Glen E. Friedman, lettering by Eric Haze

261   **Beastie Boys**
Bees Tea Boys; 1992
Note: Artwork by Todd James (REAS), lettering by Eric Haze

262   Beastie Boys
Check Your Head / Cabin; 1992
Note: Photo by Glen E. Friedman

263   Beastie Boys
"Get It Together"; 1994

264   Beastie Boys
One Two, Oh My God promo; 1994

265   Beastie Boys
Aloha Mr. Hand ringer; 1994

266   Beastie Boys
Ill Communication ringer; 1994

267   Beastie Boys
Mics of Fury ringer; 1994

House of Pain
"Top o' the Morning to Ya"; 1992

Another favorite shirt of mine was the classic House Of Pain Fine Malt Lyrics tee. It was funny, I liked the play on Mickey's big mouth beer. Only white Irish knuckleheads would know what that was. — Dante Ross

269 House of Pain
    "Come and Get Some of This"; 1992

270 House of Pain
    Liquor Store World Tour; 1993
    Note: Artwork by Frank Kozik

271 House Of Pain
    The Mean Green Machine; Early 90s
    Note: Artwork by Coop

272   Mobstyle
Goin' Out Mobstyle; Early 90s

273   Apache
"Gangsta Bitch"; 1993

274   Apache
"Kill D'White People..." promo; 1993

275   Onyx
Bacdafucup; 1993

276   Onyx
All We Got Iz Us; 1995

277   Lords of the Underground
Here Come the Lords; 1993

278 **Wu-Tang Clan**
Ain't Nuttin to Fuck Wit!; Mid 90s

279 **Wu-Tang Clan**
Wu-Wear Inc.; 1995

280 **Wu-Tang Clan**
Mid 90s

281 **Wu-Tang Clan**
"C.R.E.A.M."; Mid 90s

282 Wu-Tang Clan
Wu-Tang Forever, 1997

283 Wu-Tang Clan
Wu-Tang Forever promo; 1997

284 Wu-Tang Clan
Wu-Tang Forever, 1997

285 Wu-Tang Clan
"C.R.E.A.M."; 1997

286 Wu-Tang Clan
Promo; Mid 90s

287 Method Man
Logo; Mid 90s

288 GZA
Logo; Mid 90s

289 Wu-Tang Clan
"C.R.E.A.M."; Mid 90s

290 Wu-Tang Clan
36 Chambers of Death bootleg; Mid 90s

291 Wu-Tang Clan
Enter the Wu-Tang bootleg; Mid 90s

292   Genius / Method Man
Liquid Swords bootleg; Mid 90s

293   Raekwon
"Glaciers of Ice" bootleg; Mid 90s

294   Ghostface Killah
Ironman bootleg; Mid 90s

295   Method Man
"Bring the Pain" bootleg; Mid 90s

296   Wu-Tang Clan
Shadow Boxing bootleg; Mid 90s

297   Wu-Tang Clan / Killarmy
Bootleg; Mid 90s

298   Ol' Dirty Bastard / Mariah Carey
"Fantasy" bootleg; Mid 90s

299   Jodeci / Raekwon
"Freek 'N You" bootleg; Mid 90s

300   Method Man / Mary J. Blige
"You're All I Need" bootleg; Mid 90s

301   Nas
Illmatic promo; 1994

302 Nas
Illmatic promo hoodie; 1994

303 Nas
It Was Written promo; 1996

304 Nas
Illmatic bootleg; Mid 90s

305 Nas
"It Ain't Hard to Tell" bootleg; Mid 90s

306 Nas
"It Ain't Hard to Tell" bootleg; Mid 90s

307 Nas
"If I Ruled the World" bootleg; Mid 90s

308 Nas
"If I Ruled the World" bootleg; Mid 90s

309 Nas
"Street Dreams" bootleg; Mid 90s

310 AZ
"Sugar Hill" promo; 1995

311 AZ
"Sugar Hill" bootleg; 1995

312 Foxy Brown
"Get Me Home" / "Ill Na Na" bootleg; Mid 90s

313   Foxy Brown / The Firm
Bootleg; 1997

314   Trackmasters
Football jersey; late 90s
Note: These jerseys were made for Trackmasters (Poke & Tone) and Steve Stoute.

315　**Mobb Deep**
"Shook Ones" bootleg; 1995

Chi Modu
Mobb Deep; 1995
Opposite Page

In terms of the bootleg t-shirts that have used some of my iconic photos, I've actually always appreciated it. Those shirts were just created by local guys all over the world trying to make a couple bucks. I've seen them from New York to Nigeria, and the shirts with my photos have actually helped my brand to grow. It's a very hip-hop way of getting your images out there.
— Chi Modu, photographer

316   Mobb Deep
Bootleg; Mid 90s

317   Mobb Deep
The Infamous promo; 1995

318   Mobb Deep
Murda Muzik promo; 1999

319   Loud Records / Starter
Promo satin jacket; Late 90s

320 Slick Rick
Behind Bars promo; 1994

321 Keith Murray
The Most Beautifullest Thing in This World promo; 1994

322 Fugees
"Nappy Heads" bootleg; 1995

323   Fugees
The Score; 1996

324   Busta Rhymes
"Woo-Hah!" bootleg; 1996

325   Busta Rhymes
"Woo-Hah!" bootleg; 1996

326 Stretch Armstrong & Bobbito Show
Echo Unlimited collaboration; 1996

327 Big L
Lifestylez ov da Poor & Dangerous promo; 1995

328 Fat Joe
Jealous One's Envy promo; 1995

329   Big Pun
Capital Punishment promo; 1998

330   Cru
Da Dirty 30 promo; 1997
Note: Logo design by Cey Adams

331   Black Star
Mos Def & Talib Kweli Are Black Star promo; 1998

T. Eric Monroe
Lil' Cease, Tupac Shakur, Notorious B.I.G., and entourage
New York City; 1993

332 Bad Boy Entertainment
I'm a Bad Boy! promo; Mid 90s

333 Bad Boy Entertainment
Artist roster promo; Mid 90s

334 Bad Boy Entertainment
Million Man March; 1995

335 Craig Mack / Bad Boy Entertainment
"Flava In Ya Ear" promo; 1994

336 Craig Mack
"Can I Get Down" bootleg; Mid 90s

337 Notorious B.I.G.
Bootleg; Mid 90s

338   Notorious B.I.G. / Bad Boy Entertainment
I'm Not Only a Client... promo; 1995

339   Notorious B.I.G.
"Sky's the Limit"; Late 90s/early 2000s
Note: Produced by Brooklyn Mint, Notorious B.I.G.'s clothing line

340   Notorious B.I.G.
Ready to Die / "Big Poppa" bootleg; 1995

341 Notorious B.I.G.
Memorial; 1997

342 Notorious B.I.G.
Memorial; 1997

343 Notorious B.I.G.
Memorial; 1997

344 **Notorious B.I.G.**
Memorial; Late 90s

345 **Notorious B.I.G.**
Bootleg; Late 90s

346 **Notorious B.I.G.**
Memorial bootleg; Late 90s

347   Notorious B.I.G.
       Memorial bootleg; Late 90s

348   Notorious B.I.G.
       Memorial bootleg; Late 90s

349   Notorious B.I.G.
       Memorial bootleg; Late 90s

350　Junior M.A.F.I.A.
　　"Get Money" bootleg; 1995

351　Lil' Kim
　　Hard Core; 1996

352   Lil' Kim
"No Time" bootleg; 1996

353   Puff Daddy
Hilfiger logo; 1997

354   Puff Daddy
"All About the Benjamins"; 1997

355   Puff Daddy & The Family
No Way Out tour; 1997

356   Mase
1997

357   Mase
"Feel So Good" bootleg; Late 90s

Jonathan Mannion
Jay Z
New York City; 1996

358 Jay Z / Roc-A-Fella

Reasonable Doubt varsity jacket; 1996

Note: Courtesy of Lenny S.

Receiving the Roc-A-Fella Records jacket in '96 meant EVERYTHING to me, literally. I had never wanted to be down with an organization or crew this much, ever in life. I unfortunately didn't attend college so Roc was my fraternity. This was my letterman jacket. I felt a part of something big. I knew Jay and this label would be successful. I knew we would make history one day. All of that pride, respect, hope, and dreams were embodied in that jacket. — Lenny "Lenny S." Santiago, SVP A&R Roc Nation

359   Jay Z
Roc-A-Fella promo; 1996

360   Roc-A-Fella
Leather varsity jacket; Late 90s

361   Jay Z
Vol. 2... Hard Knock Life; 1998

362   Jay Z
Bootleg; Late 90s

363   Jay Z
"In My Lifetime" bootleg; Late 90s

364   Jay Z
"Hard Knock Life" bootleg; Late 90s

365   Jay Z / Ruff Ryders
Hard Knock Life / Ryde or Die tour; 1999

366   DMX
"Get At Me Dog" bootleg; Late 90s

367   Ruff Ryders
Ryde or Die Vol. 1; 1999

368   Ruff Ryders
Bootleg; Late 90s

369   The LOX / Ruff Ryders
"Wild Out"; 1999

370   Ruff Ryders
Artist roster leather jacket; Late 90s

371 *Rapatron '87*
Little Rock, Arkansas; 1987

372   Luke Skyywalker Records

Varsity jacket; Late 80s

My nickname as a DJ was Luke Skyywalker. I wanted a logo to describe what and who I was, so a man walking in the sky with blue jeans on described me.
— Luther "Uncle Luke" Campbell, 2 Live Crew

373 2 Live Crew
"Throw the D" / *Holiday Def Fest*; 1986

374 2 Live Crew
"D"-Tour; Mid 80s

375 2 Live Crew
"Me So Horny"; 1989

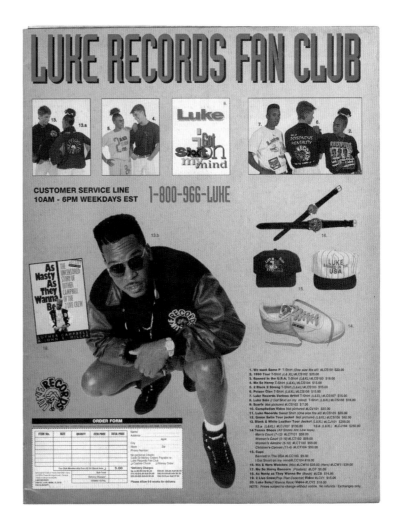

376   2 Live Crew

"2 Black 2 Strong 2 Live"; 1990

Note: In 1990, Luther Campbell was forced to stop using the Luke
Skyywalker name after a trademark lawsuit with George Lucas.

377   Luke Records Fan Club

Order form; Early 90s

Janette Beckman
2 Live Crew, New York
1990

378   Censorship Is Un-American
Early 90s

379   2 Live Crew
Banned in the U.S.A.; 1990

380   2 Live Crew
Banned in the U.S.A. tour; 1990

381 Luke
"Cowards In Compton"; 1993

People in Miami loved this shirt because there was a beef between myself and Dr. Dre and Snoop. The saying originally came from "Cowards in Broward," but when the beef happened I changed it to Compton. — Luther "Uncle Luke" Campbell

382 Luke
In the Nude; 1993

383   Luke
I Got Sh*t on My Mind; 1992

384   2 Live Crew
As Nasty As They Wanna Be bootleg; Early 90s

385   The New 2 Live Crew
"We Want Some Pussy"; Early 90s

386   Geto Boys
"Mind Playing Tricks On Me" promo; 1991

387   Geto Boys
"Crooked Officer" promo; 1993

388   Geto Boys
"6 Feet Deep" promo; 1993

389   Rap-A-Lot Records
Billboard #1 Indie Rap Label promo; 1993

390   Scarface
Mr. Scarface Is Back promo; 1991

391   Scarface
The Diary promo; 1994

392   Scarface
The Untouchable promo; 1997

393   5th Ward Boys
Gangsta Funk promo; 1994

394   Success-N-Effect
Early 90s

395   Outkast
Southernplayalisticadillacmuzik promo; 1994

396 Kriss Kross
Bootleg; Early 90s

397 So So Def Bass All-Stars
"Whatz Up, Whatz Up" / Freaknik '95 promo; 1995

398 Master P
Ghetto Dope promo; 1997

399 Master P
Ghetto D promo; 1997

400 Master P
"Is There a Heaven For a Gangsta?" promo; 1997

401 **Silkk the Shocker**
Charge It 2 Da Game promo; 1998

402 **No Limit Records**
We Can't Be Stopped promo; 1998

403   Master P
Bootleg; Late 90s

404   No Limit Soldiers / Master P
Bootleg; Late 90s

405   Master P
Bootleg; Late 90s

406　Master P
Bootleg; Late 90s

407　Master P
Bootleg; Late 90s

408　504 Boyz / No Limit
Bootleg; Late 90s

409   Mystikal
Big Boy Records promo; 1994

410   Three 6 Mafia
Chapter 2: World Domination promo; 1997

411   Big Tymers
How You Luv That promo; 1998

412   Juvenile
400 Degreez bootleg; 1998

413   Juvenile / Cash Money
"Back That Thang Up" bootleg; 1998

414   Hot Boy$
Guerilla Warfare bootleg; 1999

415   Bone Thugs-n-Harmony
"1st Of Tha Month" bootleg; 1995

416   Bone Thugs-n-Harmony
Mid 90s

417   Bone Thugs-n-Harmony
Ruthless to the Bone tour; 1996–97

418   Bone Thugs-n-Harmony
"Crossroads" bootleg; 1995

419   LA Dream Team
Kings of the West Coast, 1985

420   Ice-T
Power bootleg; 1988

421   Ice-T
Power bootleg; 1988
Opposite Page

422   Ice-T / Rhyme Syndicate
The Iceberg tour; 1989

423   Ice-T / Rhyme Syndicate
Australian tour; 1989

424   Ice-T / Rhyme Syndicate
The Iceberg Canadian tour; 1990
Note: Signed by Ice-T, Afrika Islam, Donald D., Evil E. and others

425   Ice-T / Rhyme Syndicate
World tour; 1990

426   Ice-T
The Iceberg; 1989
Note: Artwork by Devious Doze AKA Doze Green

427   Ice-T
The Iceberg / Freedom of Speech; 1989

428   Rhyme Syndicate Productions
Late 80s

429   Ice-T
O.G. Original Gangster, 1991

430   Ice-T
O.G. Original Gangster; 1991

431   Ice-T
O.G. Original Gangster; 1991

432   Ice-T / Body Count
O.G. Original Gangster world tour; 1991

433   Parental Advisory Explicit Lyrics
Late 80s
Note: Ice-T's *Rhyme Pays* (1987) was the first hip-hop album to have a Parental Advisory sticker

434   Ice-T
Home Invasion; 1993

435 Ice-T
World tour; Early 90s

436 West Coast Rap All-Stars
"We're All in the Same Gang"; 1990

437　*Rap Jam '91*
1991

438　Too Short
Life Is...Too Short promo hoodie; 1989

439   Too Short
Short Dog's In the House tour; 1990

440   Digital Underground
Sex Packets promo; 1990

441   Digital Underground
"The Humpty Dance"; 1990

442   Digital Underground
Sex Packets / "Humpty Dance" promo; 1990

443   Delicious Vinyl
Late 80s
Note: Delicious Vinyl logo by Eric Haze

444   Delicious Vinyl
Varsity jacket; Late 80s
Note: Courtesy of Eric Haze

445   Tone Loc
"Wild Thing"; 1989

446   Young M.C.
Stone Cold Rhymin'; 1989

447 *Eazy Duz It* Tour
1989

448   Eazy-E
Eazy Duz It bootleg; Late 80s

449   N.W.A & D.J. Eazy-E
Bootleg; Early 90s

450   Eazy-E
Tour; 1989

451   Eazy-E
"We Want Eazy" bootleg; Late 80s

452　N.W.A
Straight Outta Compton bootleg; Late 80s

453　N.W.A
Straight Outta Compton promo; 1989

454 N.W.A
Straight Outta Compton bootleg; Late 80s

455 N.W.A
"F*** the Police"; Late 80s

456 N.W.A
1991

457   Eazy-E & N.W.A
1990

458   N.W.A
100 Miles and Runnin'; 1990

459   N.W.A
"Just Don't Bite It"; 1990

460 N.W.A
EFIL4ZAGGIN; 1991

461 N.W.A
EFIL4ZAGGIN; 1991

462 N.W.A
EFIL4ZAGGIN; 1991

463 Eazy-E
1992

464 Eazy-E
It's On (Dr. Dre) 187um Killa; 1993

465 Priority Records
America's Most Wanted; Mid 90s

466　Ice Cube
AmeriKKKas Most Wanted; 1990

467　Priority Records
Mid 90s

468　Ice Cube
Mid 90s

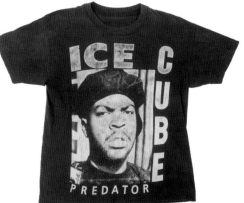

469   Ice Cube
1992

470   Ice Cube
The Predator bootleg; 1992

471   Ice Cube
Lethal Injection promo; 1993

472   Ice Cube
"Check Yo Self" bootleg; 1992

473   Ice Cube
Strictly 40's bootleg; Early 90s

474   St. Ides / Street Knowledge Productions
1992

475 Casual
Fear Itself; Mid 90s

476 Del Tha Funkee Homosapien
Late 90s

477 Souls of Mischief
Late 90s

478   The Pharcyde
Where's Quinton?; 1992

479   The Pharcyde
1993

480   Funkdoobiest
Which Doobie U B?; 1993.

481   Cypress Hill
1991

482   Cypress Hill
1991

483   Cypress Hill
1992

484   Cypress Hill
Blunted; 1995

485   Cypress Hill
1993

486   Dr. Dre
The Chronic bootleg; 1994

487   Dr. Dre
The Chronic / "Deeez Nuuuts"; 1993

488   Dr. Dre
In Bud We Trust; 1994
Note: Artwork by Pushead

489   Dr. Dre
The Chronic; 1994
Note: Artwork by Pushead

490   Dr. Dre
Helter Skelter; Mid 90s
Note: Unreleased album

491   Snoop Doggy Dogg
Beware Of Dogg; 1993

492   Snoop Doggy Dogg
Doggystyle; 1993

493 Snoop Doggy Dogg
"What's My Name"; 1993

494 Snoop Doggy Dogg
"Gin & Juice"; 1994

495 Snoop Doggy Dogg
Murder Was the Case; 1994

496   Snoop Doggy Dogg
"Gin & Juice" CCM hockey jersey; 1994

497 **Snoop Doggy Dogg**
Doggystyle bootleg; Mid 90s

498 **Snoop Doggy Dogg**
"What's My Name" bootleg; Mid 90s

499 **Snoop Doggy Dogg**
"Gin & Juice" bootleg; Mid 90s

500 **Warren G**
Regulate...G Funk Era; 1994

501 **Warren G**
"This DJ"; 1994

502 **Warren G**
"Regulate" bootleg; Mid 90s

503   2Pac
"I Get Around" bootleg; mid-90s

504   2Pac
1997

505   2Pac
Makaveli; Late 90s

506   2Pac & Snoop Doggy Dogg
      "How Do U Want It" bootleg; Mid 90s

507   2Pac / Patra
      "Dear Mama" bootleg; Mid 90s

508   2Pac
      Bootleg; Mid 90s

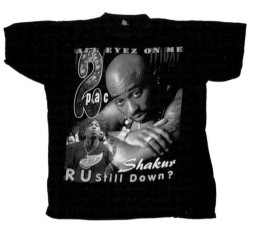

509   2Pac
"So Many Tears" bootleg; Late 90s

510   2Pac
All Eyez On Me bootleg; Late 90s

511   2Pac
Memorial bootleg; Late 90s

512   2Pac & Notorious B.I.G.
      Memorial bootleg; Late 90s

513   2Pac & Notorious B.I.G.
      Memorial bootleg; Late 90s

514   2Pac & Notorious B.I.G.
      Memorial bootleg; Late 90s

Charlie Ahearn
Wild Style Japan premiere (Busy Bee in *Wild Style* shirt, with Afrika Islam and K.K. Rockwell)
Japan; 1983

515 *Breakin'*
1984

516 *Breakin' II: Electric Boogaloo*
1984

517 *Beat Street*
1984

518   40 Acres and a Mule / Spike's Joint
Baseball jersey; Mid 90s

519   *Do the Right Thing*
1989

520   *Do the Right Thing*
       1989

521   *Do the Right Thing*
       1989

522   *Do the Right Thing*
       Mookie; 1989

523 *She's Gotta Have It*
1986

524 *Jungle Fever*
1991

525 *Jungle Fever*
1991

526   *Clockers*
1995

527　*Boyz N the Hood*
1991
Note: Logo design by Brent Rollins

528　*Boyz N the Hood*
Bootleg; 1991

529 *Boyz N the Hood*
1991

530 *Boyz N the Hood*
Bootleg; 1991

531 *Boyz N the Hood*
1991

532 *Boyz N the Hood*
Bootleg; 1991

533 *Poetic Justice*
1993
Note: Logo design by Brent Rollins

534 *New Jack City*
1991

535 *Menace II Society*
1993

536 *Juice*
1992

537 *Above the Rim*
1994

538 *Juice*
1992

539   *CB4*
1993

540   *I'm Gonna Git You Sucka*
1988

541 *Friday*
1995

T-SHIRT CONTRIBUTORS

Akihiko (Gunyara)
218, 226, 231, 249, 273, 290, 330, 335, 394, 452, 453, 460, 476, 502

Bill Adler (eyejammie.com)
007, 017, 026, 041, 086, 128

Brent Rollins (brentrollins.com)
247

Brian Procell (procell.nyc)
063, 109, 113, 121, 143, 145, 208, 216, 221, 239, 250, 260, 263, 265, 266, 267, 270, 271, 274, 282, 284, 288, 292, 309, 313, 320, 324, 337, 349, 350, 400, 406, 426, 449, 479, 480, 483, 484, 503, 504, 506, 507, 513, 514, 525, 533

Chapel NYC
036, 055, 153, 182, 280, 347, 396, 405, 425, 456, 510

Daniel Ladd
002, 012, 031, 039, 074, 134, 184, 196, 326, 423, 540

Dave Tompkins
372

DJ Alamaki
016, 133, 148, 338, 385, 451, 455, 497, 528, 530, 539

DJ Kango
043, 048, 069, 172, 204, 286, 383, 386

DJ Ken-Ske
277, 472

DJ Kitta
194, 305, 440

DJ Koya
011, 018, 061, 130, 136, 138

DJ Ross One
005, 006, 008, 009, 010, 014, 015, 019, 021, 022, 023, 024, 029, 030, 032, 035, 037, 040, 046, 050, 051, 052, 056, 058, 068, 077, 079, 081, 083, 085, 087, 090, 091, 092, 093, 096, 097, 099, 101, 102, 103, 104, 105, 106, 108, 110, 116, 118, 119, 122, 125, 127, 135, 137, 141, 142, 147, 151, 152, 154, 156, 158, 161, 162, 164, 165, 167, 169, 170, 171, 175, 177, 178, 179, 185, 187, 188, 190, 191, 192, 195, 197, 198, 199, 200, 201, 203, 206, 207, 211, 213, 217, 219, 220, 222, 223, 227, 229, 232, 233, 234, 235, 237, 240, 241, 244, 246, 248, 252, 253, 254, 255, 256, 258, 261, 262, 275, 279, 283, 285, 287, 289, 291, 293, 296, 298, 299, 301, 303, 304, 307, 310, 311, 314, 315, 316, 317, 318, 319, 321, 322, 323, 329, 331, 333, 339, 340, 341, 342, 343, 351, 352, 353, 354, 355, 356, 359, 360, 361, 362, 363, 364, 365, 367, 369, 371, 373, 374, 375, 376, 378, 380, 381, 387, 389, 390, 391, 392, 397, 398, 401, 402, 408, 409, 410, 411, 412, 413, 414, 415, 417, 421, 422, 424, 428, 430, 431, 433, 434, 435, 436, 437, 447, 458, 465, 467, 469, 471, 473, 474, 475, 478, 485, 490, 491, 495, 505, 512, 515, 517, 519, 520, 521, 522, 523, 524, 526, 532, 534, 537, 538

DJ Yuke
382, 384, 388, 536

Eli Escobar
044, 073, 114, 115

Eric Haze (interhaze.com)
065, 098, 159, 444

GANszok
155, 327

Graham Funke
264

Harley Viera-Newton
238

IseeRobots (iseerobots.com)
107

Janette Beckman (janettebeckman.com)
027

Jeff "Chairman" Mao (egotripland.com)
168

John Paddick
140, 181, 228

Kaminaccho
095, 132, 193, 306

KCD (BBPBX.com)
020, 045, 174, 180, 212, 215, 230

Ken-Row
059, 060, 066, 080

Kevin Scott (djkevinscott.com)
025, 062, 071, 084, 094, 117, 257, 268, 269, 278, 281, 345, 419, 427, 432, 445, 446, 461, 466, 468, 481, 486, 487, 492, 493, 501, 516, 527, 529, 531, 541

Kirk Tilton / For All To Envy (foralltoenvy.com)
028, 033, 034, 038, 042, 049, 053, 054, 057, 064, 067, 070, 072, 075, 076, 100, 120, 123, 124, 131, 144, 146, 149, 150, 166, 183, 189, 205, 210, 214, 243, 251, 259, 276, 294, 295, 297, 300, 302, 308, 312, 332, 334, 336, 344, 346, 348, 366, 368, 370, 395, 399, 403, 404, 418, 420, 429, 439, 448, 450, 454, 457, 459, 462, 463, 464, 470, 482, 494, 496, 498, 500, 508, 509, 511, 518, 535

Kohji "K-Prince" Maruyama (BBPBX.com)
003

Lenny "Lenny S." Santiago
358

Mike Hastings
357, 407

Monk One
225

Newtype Online (newtypeonlineshop.net)
111, 112, 186

Panzo aka Pee-Fine (yobrospro.buyshop.jp)
126, 139, 157, 160, 173, 176, 272, 328, 438, 499

Poor K. (yobrospro.buyshop.jp)
004, 013, 082, 089

Raul Sanchez
377

Sarah Honda
416

Sean Kinney
209

Showbiz (ditcent.com)
224

Stretch Armstrong
163

Takuya & Taku (portration.com)
047, 078, 088, 129, 202, 236, 242, 245, 379, 441, 442, 443, 477, 488, 489

What Goes Around Comes Around
(whatgoesaroundnyc.com)
001

Zen La Rock
325, 393

PHOTOGRAPHERS

Cathy Campbell
Charlie Ahearn (charlieahearn.com)
Chi Modu (chimodu.com)
Glen E. Friedman (burningflags.com)
Janette Beckman (janettebeckman.com)
Joe Conzo (joeconzo.com)
Jonathan Mannion (jonathanmannion.com)
Peter Nash aka Prime Minister Pete Nice
Ricky Powell (rickypowell.com)
T. Eric Monroe

THE AUTHOR

Ross Schwartzman aka DJ Ross One is a Cincinnati born DJ and collector of all things hip-hop. Armed with a MFA in Photography from the School of Visual Arts, he promptly chose DJing as a full time career and now resides between New York City and Miami. A self-proclaimed "rap nerd", Ross has been collecting hip-hop ephemera and memorabilia since age 15. Whether it be classic boomboxes, records, early party flyers, or t-shirts, his passion for the music and the hunt for these relics has led him to accumulate some of the coolest rap-related items in the world.

djrossone.com

ACKNOWLEDGEMENTS

First and foremost thank you to all of the shirt contributors and photographers listed.

Additional thanks to: Michael & Dawn Schwartzman, Harley Viera-Newton, Pres Rodriguez, Davey Urfman, Alyssa Ender, Craig Cohen, Will Luckman, Wes Del Val, Cey Adams, Eric Haze, Brent Rollins, Bill Adler, Russell Simmons, Rick Rubin, Rev Run, DJ Red Alert, L.L. Cool J, DJ Jazzy Jeff, Pete Nash, Hiro Numata, Erin Heatherton, Bill Spector, Brian Procell, Kirk Tilton, Kevin & Joy Scott, Tony Arcabascio, Z-Trip, Dante Ross, Ayanna Wilks, Stephanie Nash, Ashley Newton, Raul Sanchez, Brian Merriam, Lenny S., Big Sean, Stretch Armstrong, Lyle Owerko, Jeremie at A-1, Jeff Henrikson, Chris Black, Yoni Goldberg, Michael Gardner, Dave Grutman, Cedric Walker, DJ Riz, DJ MOS, Derrick "D-Nice" Jones, Corey Shapiro, Andy "Roctakon" Brown, Rhasaan Orange, DJ 7L, Jun "Tea Kato" Ohki, Exe, Shoki, Jake One, DJ Cipher, KeepItReal Vintage, Jonathan "Shecky Green" Shecter, Paul Mittleman, Tono Radvany, Claudine Joseph, Edith Bo, Christina Thomas, Zan & Mo

Rap Tees:
A Collection of Hip-Hop T-Shirts 1980–1999

Text, editing, and compilation © 2015 DJ Ross One
T-Shirt Photography: DJ Ross One
Art Direction: Pres Rodriguez
Design: Pres Rodriguez and DJ Ross One
Additional Introduction copy editing: Michael King

Published in the United States by powerHouse Books,
a division of powerHouse Cultural Entertainment, Inc.
32 Adams Street, Brooklyn, NY 11201, USA

www.powerHouseBooks.com

First edition, 2015

Library of Congress Control Number: 2015946258

ISBN 978-1-57687-775-3

10 9 8 7 6 5 4

Printing and binding by Pimlico Book International

Printed and bound in China